101 Amazing Things to Do in Budapest

D1742132

Introduction

So you're going to Budapest, huh? You are very lucky indeed! You are sure in for a treat because Budapest is truly one of the most magical cities on this planet. There's a mix of incredible architecture, awesome restaurants and cafes, and amazing nightlife and shopping that makes Budapest one of the most enduringly popular tourist destinations on the earth.

In this guide, we'll be giving you the low down on:
- the very best things to shove in your pie hole, from street food staples to gourmet restaurants
- the best shopping so that you can take a little piece of Budapest back home with you
- incredible festivals, whether you're into local culture or dancing to banging electronic music
- the coolest historical and cultural sights that you simply cannot afford to miss
- where to party like someone from Budapest and make local friends
- and tonnes more coolness besides!

Let's not waste any more time – here are the 101 most amazing, spectacular, and coolest things not to miss in Budapest!

1. Dance Your Socks off at the Bangin' Sziget Festival

One of the best things about Europe during the summer is the European festival circuit, and if you haven't yet been to Sziget Festival in Budapest, you seriously need to make it your festival priority for the summer. This festival takes over 102 hectares of land on an island in the middle of the Danube, and there are over 1000 performances over the course of the festival! From banging electronic and rock music, to circus performances and kids' activities, there is something for everyone at Sziget.

(http://szigetfestival.com)

2. Explore Traditional Hungarian Life at Budapest's Ethnography Museum

There is more to Budapest than cute coffee shops and beautiful architecture, and you can explore the folk traditions of Budapest and Hungary when you visit this fascinating museum. The permanent exhibition features a collection of more than 3000 items, including manuscripts, handicrafts, bridal dresses, cooking utensils, and more besides.

(Budapest, Kossuth Lajos tér 12; www.neprajz.hu)

3. Immerse Yourself in Culture at the Budapest Summer Festival

Budapest is a city of culture, and this is never more evident than during the summer festival, which typically takes place between July and August. During the festival, you can catch open air theatre productions and concerts in Budapest's parks, special boat cruises on the Danube river, pop-up art exhibitions, and even stand-up comedy shows. *(http://eng.szabadter.hu)*

4. Allow Your Stomach to Become Acquainted with Chimney Cake

If you have a sweet tooth, you are in luck, because Budapest is absolutely jam packed full of bakeries and confectioners. One of the local treats is called a kurto kalacs, or chimney cake in English. This is essentially a cylinder or sweet dough that is roasted to give it a golden brown finish, and it's then rolled in sugar and sometimes cinnamon. Yummy.

5. Have Fun Ice Skating on City Park Lake

Budapest is one of those wonderful European cities that has an abundance of greens space where you can breathe some fresh air. The most popular is probably City Park, which contains a zoo, a palace, museums, and lots of green space. But the highlight has to be the peaceful lake, which during the winter months is transformed into an ice skating rink, and nothing beats the fun of sipping on hot chocolate and zipping around an open air ice rink with close friends.

(Kós Károly stny)

6. Enjoy Classical Music in Hungary's National Concert Hall

Among all of the traditional buildings in Budapest, there is one more contemporary building that really stands out among the older structures, and that's the Bela Bartok National Concert Hall, which was only designed and constructed this century. Although it is a new building, the interior has the feel of a Gothic cathedral, with acoustics that are every bit as impressive. Classical music concerts are hosted here throughout the year, and catching one is sure to be a memorable experience.

(Komor Marcell utca 1; www.mupa.hu/en)

7. Gorge on Baked Goods in a 19th Century Cafe

There are plenty of places in Budapest where you can sit down with a strong cup of coffee and a slice of cake, but there is nowhere quite as special as Ruszwurm. This café is special because it's a 200 year old family business! Inside, it's super quaint, and you shouldn't leave before tucking into their specialty, the Zserbo cake, which is a sweet treat made from strawberries and cottage cheese – perfect for a Budapest summer's day.

(Szentháromság u. 7; www.ruszwurm.hu)

8. Explore the Ruinpubs of the City's 7th District

When you explore any new city, it's a good idea to move away from the city centre and explore some of the outer suburbs. One of the local neighbourhoods to visit in Budapest is District 7, if only for its famous Ruinpubs. Ruinpubs are actually a fairly recent Budapest phenomenon. Old derelict buildings that were doomed for destruction were converted into pubs and filled with furniture from old community centres, cinemas, and granny flats, giving them a very distinct feel. There are tours of the Ruinpubs that you can join, but a few of the best are Szimpla Kert, Fogas Haz, and Innio Borbar.

9. Treat Yourself to Some Traditional Hungarian Porcelain

Walk along the streets of Budapest and you will soon realise that this is a city where there is a really vibrant arts, crafts, and design culture. One of the most famous crafts to emerge from Budapest is its stunning porcelain. Herend porcelain is probably the most famous porcelain brand in the city, well known for its particular patterns and for being hand painted. There are a few Herend Porcelain shops where you can treat yourself, and you might even want to visit the Herend Porcelain factory.
(http://herend.com/information)

10. Embrace Hungarian Design at WAMP Design Fair

Once a month, this design market pops up at Erzsebet Square, showcasing the wares of carefully selected local designers. This is 100% the place to get to grips with Budapest's impressive creative scene, and to take something truly original home with you. Design work on display includes leather gloves makers, hand bound books, hand crafted jewellery, original prints, and much more besides.

(http://wamp.hu/en)

11. Get Romantic at The Tree of Love Locks

Visiting Budapest as a couple? Well, you're in luck because this is the perfect place to feel all lovey dovey with your significant other. In fact, you can find love locks all over the city. One such place is The Tree of Love Locks in Elisabeth Square. Customising your own lock and placing it lovingly in the park is a great way to cement a memorable romantic trip between the two of you.

12. Weave Your Own Scarf at a Traditional Shop

As you walk along the streets of Budapest, your eyes might be taken by the beautiful textiles that the women wear, particularly patterned scarfs. Of course, it's a great idea to go scarf shopping while in the city, but you can do one better at the **Belvárosi Szövöde** weaving mill and weave a scarf of your very own. Pick out the colours and design, and the friendly staff will walk you through the whole process. Talk about a unique memory of Budapest to take home with you.

(Dob u. 22)

13. Take a Walking Tour of Jewish Budapest

There are numerous walking tours that can help you to learn about the city on foot, and the most impressive is certainly the tour of Jewish Budapest. Extremely knowledgeable guides will take you through the history of the Jewish population before, during, and after the Second World War, and the effect the war had on the local Jewish population. The Jewish district is slightly outside of the centre so this is a chance to explore the city from more of a local perspective.

14. Take a Painting Class at Art School Budapest

Perhaps you are the kind of person who really likes to get stuck into activities instead of wandering around museums and galleries all day, in which case, the perfect Budapest treat is to enrol in a painting class or even a whole course at Budapest ART Factory. This is one for real art enthusiasts who really want to learn their craft because this is a practicing art studio where local artists also exhibit their work.

(Váci út 152; www.budapestartfactory.com)

15. Discover Emerging Hungarian Art at INDA Galeria

To say that there is a strong gallery culture in Budapest would be a grand understatement. You could actually spend a whole week hopping from gallery to gallery if you are an art lover, which is not a bad idea in the slightest. Of course, there are the major galleries, but there are also lots of "up and coming" hole in the wall type places, and INDA Galeria is one that is well worth a visit. This gallery is committed to showcasing new works from local artists so you can really get a sense of Budapest's contemporary art scene there.

(Király u. 34; http://indagaleria.hu/en)

16. Get Festive at the Christmas Market in Vörösmarty Square

If there is one time of year to plan a trip to Budapest, it's undoubtedly the run up to Christmas. The picturesque city becomes even more beautiful with a dousing of snow and twinkling Christmas decorations, and there are multiple Christmas markets where you can buy gifts and drink mulled wine as well. The market in Vörösmarty Square is particularly special, with delicious treats like roasted goose thigh and honey cookies, and fun activities the whole family can take part in.

17. Watch Open Air Theatre in Margaret Island

Margaret Island is a floating island of green in the centre of the city with many attractions, and one of the most popular is the open air stage where plays are performed as part of the Budapest Summer Festival when the city experiences milder evenings. And this isn't some pop-up stage with a small audience – the theatre can accommodate up to 3500 guests, and the productions staged there are really lavish! Definitely one foe arts and theatre lovers not to miss.

18. Enjoy the View From Gellert Hill

Something that you can see on Budapest's skyline no matter where you are in the city is the local Statue of Liberty. Many people don't realise that they can actually get up close to the statue with a brisk hike up Gellert Hill. This is a lovely green walk for nature lovers, and at the top of the hill there is an incredible view of the whole of Budapest. On your way down, relax in the thermal Gellet Baths to rest your tired muscles following the hike.

19. Take the Coghill Railway Through Buda Hills

Would you board a train that is totally run by kids? Well, that's exactly what you could be doing in Budapest! This train line was built after the Second World War as a way to test the skills of local kids and get them to work as a team – and it still exists and is operational today! The kids take their jobs super seriously, and you'll catch some beautiful scenery as you chug through.

20. Sip on Mulled Wine and Go Sledding at Normafa

Budapest is one of the greatest cities in Europe for winter activities. One of the most fun things you can do is head to Normafa Hill, which at 45 minutes outside of the downtown area, will give you an opportunity to escape the tourists. In the winter months, there is organised sledding, which is huge amounts of fun no matter your age. And there is a chalet on the hill where you can also treat yourself to a steaming cup of mulled wine.

21. Fight the Meat Sweats at Meat Boutique

Looking to indulge your inner carnivore on your trip to Budapest? Well, of course you are! And there is only one place to do so whole hog (excuse the pun), and that's at Meat Boutique. Whether you want a gigantic piece of steak or the very best burger of your life, Meat Boutique gets meat lovers salivating from the moment they step inside the restaurant. And there's a stellar view of the Danube to boot!

(Lánchíd u. 7; http://meatboutique.hu)

22. Explore the City Via Tram

If you are trying to navigate your way around Budapest, you don't need to book an expensive tour. Budapest's tram system is one of the very best in Europe, and by hopping on and off tram line #2 with a one day pass, you can easily catch loads of the main tourist sights within the city, such as the Budapest Parliament, the Chain Bridge, and Vorosmarty Square. A daily tourist ticket that allows you on all the tram lines, metro, and buses is just 5 euros.

23. Take in the Majesty of Budapest's Parliament Building

Budapest's parliament is the third largest parliament building in the entire world, and to say it's a jaw dropping feat of architecture is something of an understatement. When the National Assembly isn't in session, you can also be wowed by the building's interior on a 45 minute guided tour. On the tour, you'll get to see the most impressive rooms of the building, as well as the Hungarian Crown Jewels.

(Kossuth Lajos tér 1-3; www.parlament.hu)

24. Treat Yourself to Gerbeaud Cake at Café Gerbeaud

Café Gerbeaud is an essential café on your "must-visit" list in Budapest. Before you think that you can't put another slice of cake into your mouth, you absolutely need to make an exception for the Gerbeaud cake. This rich dessert has a history of 125 years in the café, and comprises layers of walnut sponge, apricot preserve, and chocolate. Trust us when we say you'll be back for a second slice.

(www.gerbeaud.hu)

25. Celebrate a Hungarian Easter at the Easter Sheep Festival

Budapest is one of the best cities in the world for festivities and celebrations, and this is why planning an Easter vacation in Hungary is a really awesome idea. Yup, there is a sheep festival! The highlight at this festival is, of course, the sheep. Being along your little ones and they'll be able to pet the sheep as well as other domestic animals. As well as cute animals to pet, there are Easter themed workshops, traditional folk shows, and lots of local food to sample. The festival takes places in City Park.

26. Learn How to Make Chocolate Treats at Szamos Chocolate School

Who doesn't love to indulge in a bar of chocolate now and again? Well, if you want to take your chocolate appreciation to the next level, you can learn about the craft of chocolate at the famous Szamos Chocolate School in the city. You don't need any prior experience, and the expert chocolatiers will take you through the process of making delectable bon bons and chocolate truffles.

(www.csokoladeiskola.hu/ english.html)

27. Chill Out With Coffee and a Book at Alexandra Bookcafé

There are numerous cafes in Budapest where you can relax in a quaint environment, but Alexandra Bookcafé stands out from the crowd because this place doubles as a book shop. If you neglected to take any holiday reads with you on your trip to Budapest, you can stock up at the bookshop and then relax with an espresso. This café is decked out with chandeliers and a fresco style ceiling, so it's a particularly decadent place to spend a lazy afternoon in the city.

(Andrássy út 39; www.lotzterem.hu)

28. Chow Down From Food Trucks at Karavan

The food truck movement has become hugely popular across the world in the last few years, and Budapest certainly hasn't been left out. If you want to check out the city's local food truck scene, head to Karavan, a mobile food court on Kazinczy street. Here you'll be able to try every type of food under the sun, from traditional chimney cake snacks, through to international fare such as Mexican tacos and Chinese steamed buns.

(Kazinczy u. 18; www.streetfoodkaravan.hu)

29. Taste Extravagant Hungarian Dishes at Onyx Restaurant

When you are on a trip away, you'll want to treat yourself to some special food. You may not be able to afford to eat in award winning restaurants for every meal, but if you can have just one special dinner, make sure that it's at Michelin star restaurant, Onyx. At Onyx, you'll be sat on gilt chairs under glistening chandeliers, and you'll be treated to authentic Hungarian fare with a contemporary twist. Go for the tasting menu to try a range of exciting treats, and be sure to reserve a table ahead of time!

(Vörösmarty tér 7; www.onyxrestaurant.hu)

30. Hang with Hungarian Hipsters at Kolor

Want to find the hipsters of Budapest? You'll find them eating, drinking, and dancing at the city's newest "it" place, Kolor. Kolor is located within the beautiful Gozsdu Courtyard where you can make the most of the summer weather, and the bar's impressive cocktail menu. In the early evening, you can catch fun events such as screenings of art films, panel discussions, and talks from local artists. And as the hours wear on, the tunes start to spin and the beautiful people of Budapest hit the dancefloor.

(Király u. 13)

31. Connect With Nature in Hungary's Oldest Botanical Gardens

Budapest isn't really the kind of city that overwhelms people with its traffic and hustle and bustle, but even with Budapest, there might be times when you want to escape the streets and find respite in some greenery. At that moment, you head to Fuveskert Botanical Gardens, the oldest botanical gardens in all of Hungary, dating back to 1771. Open from April until October, here you will find

200 kinds of endangered plants, and a beautiful Japanese garden with cherry blossoms.

(Villányi út 29-43; https://kertk.szie.hu/karunkrol/budai-arboretum)

32. Drink and Drink Some More at Főzdefesz Craft Beer Festival

City Park isn't just a place to relax around the lake, because each year the park hosts a fantastic craft beer festival. At this festival, new-wave beer makers from up and down the country are invited to share their wares with the festival's merry makers. And, of course, there is always lots of food on offer as well, from big bowls of goulash to spicy Hungarian sausages. The festival typically takes place each June.

33. Get Cultural at the Annual Night of Museums

If it's culture that you're after, Budapest is the place for you, and the city really demonstrates what a cultural haven it is on its Annual Night of Museums, which tends to happen in June each year. On this one night of the year, some of the most well known as well as the quirkiest museums across the city stay open until 2:30am, and host some very special events and workshops. One ticket gives you access to all the museums, as well as Budapest's transport system. This is one that culture vultures shouldn't miss.

34. Take in Summer Concerts at a Hungarian Castle

Budapest is a totally different city in the winter and summer months. While it's definitely worth a visit at any time of year, if you love the idea of outdoor festivals and concerts, be sure that you visit the Hungarian capital in the summertime. One of the summer highlights is a series of concerts that takes place at Vajdahunyad castle. These are mostly classical music concerts, and the atmospheric setting truly provides a new dimension to the music. *(Vajdahunyad vár; www.vajdahunyadcastle.com)*

35. Shop Til You Drop on Budapest's Fashion Street

If your idea of a good time is to shop until you can't shop anymore, there are plenty of opportunities to bleed your credit cards dry in Budapest. The best place to start is Fashion Street. This is the street where you can find all the big brand names that you know and love, such as Max Mara, Lacoste, and Hugo Boss.

(Deák Ferenc u. 15; http://fashionstreet.hu)

36. Get Folksy at the Festival of Folk Arts in Buda Castle

A trip to Budapest offers a real opportunity to get to grips with traditional Hungarian folk cultures. The Festival of the Folk Arts is a festival hosted each year in stunning Buda Castle where you can learn about traditions from craftspeople who are invited from all over Hungary. They share their talents in everything from egg painting to wood carving, and much much more. There's also opportunity to try lots of Hungarian food, wine, and spirits, and the festival usually coincides with St Stephen's Day in August.

(www.mestersegekunnepe.hu)

37. Paint Eggs at Easter Time

One of the best times to be in Budapest is around Easter, when all kinds of festivities happen in and around the city.

One of the most traditional activities at this time is to paint eggs. And this isn't some new tradition, it actually dates back to a time before Hungary even existed as a country, as painted eggs have been dug up from Hungarian soil and date to pre-Magyar times. The annual Easter Market at the Museum of Ethnography is a great place to have some fun with this old tradition.

38. Get Art Happy at the Hungarian National Gallery

The arts culture of Budapest and Hungary is impressive to say the least, and it's at the Hungarian National Gallery that you can feel the power of the country's art culture more than anywhere else. It covers the expanse of Hungarian art across all of its genres, from Hungarian baroque to contemporary artists. And the gallery is set within the stunning Buda Castle, which is worth a visit in its own right.

(Szent György tér 2; http://mng.hu/en)

39. Sip on Hungarian Wines at Budapest Wine Festival

When you purchase a bottle of wine to eat with your evening meal, it's unlikely that you have ever picked up anything from Hungary on your walk around the supermarket, but actually, this country produces a lot of wine in its vineyards, and very good wine at that. If you fancy yourself as a bit of a wine connoisseur, you shouldn't miss Budapest's annual Wine Festival, which takes place in September every year. As well as being able to sample lots of local wine, there is also a wine auction and a selection of live performances.

40. Find Something Special at an Antique Market

Would you like to find a one-of-a-kind item in Budapest that's more valuable than a banded mug in a tourist shop? Than you should definitely head to KORZO, a fair that takes place every Sunday in Budapest, and showcases the wares of antiques dealers, as well as local Hungarian designers. You can find everything from vintage photographs of the city to hand crafted jewellery items, and much more besides. And don't forget to haggle because it's expected at this market!

41. Experience Traditional Hungary at the National Gallop

If you love nothing more than a little flutter on a horse race, you should make sure that your trip to Budapest coincides with The National Gallop. This annual event, hosted each year in September, centres around a horse race that revives Hungarian military and equestrian traditions with each horse representing a town or city in the country. The event takes place in Heroes Square, the largest square in Budapest, which gets covered in sand and transformed into a racecourse.

(http://en.vagta.hu)

42. Try Budapest's Best Goulash Soup at Hungarikum Bistro

If there is one dish that you have to try during your time in Budapest, it is goulash soup. Goulash is essentially a thick stew that is perfect for keeping your body warm during the winter months. It will often contain big chunks of beef, winter vegetables, red wine, and seasoned with paprika, nutmeg, and other warming spices. You can find goulash all over the city but Hungarikum Bistro is a local joint where it's said to be especially tasty.

(Steindl Imre u. 13; http://hungarikumbisztro.hu)

43. Relax in the Szechenyi Baths

Without a doubt, the Szechenyi Baths is one of the main reasons that tourists keep flocking to the Hungarian capital, year in and year out. Located in the City Park, in front of a stunning place, this is the largest medicinal bath in all of Europe. There are 15 indoor baths and 3 huge outdoor pools where you will find crowds at any time of the year. There are often parties hosted in the baths, but if you just want to relax and unwind, that's cool too.

(Állatkerti krt. 9-11; http://szechenyispabaths.com)

44. Chow Down on Goose Liver

Goose liver and Foie Gras is one of the best known luxury food products in Hungary, and you shouldn't leave the city without sampling your fair share of this delicacy. Kispiac Bisztro is the ideal place to try this local food, and you should also try the veal liver and the duck liver pate. And at Tigris Étterem you can order a goose liver selection plate to try goose liver in its various incarnations.

(Mérleg u. 10; www.tigrisrestaurant.hu)

45. Visit the Quirky Hospital in the Rock Museum

If you want to explore the quirkier, lesser known side of Budapest, the Hospital in the Rock Museum needs to be on your "must see" list. This museum is a 6km stretch of caves and cellars in Buda Castle Hill, and it's dedicated to a former emergency hospital and nuclear bunker. The caves and cellars were fortified to protect people from attack during the Second World War, and a hospital was also built there to treat civilians and soldiers alike.

(Lovas út 4/C; www.sziklakorhaz.eu/en)

46. Wave a Rainbow Flag for Budapest Pride

When you think of Central and Eastern Europe, you probably don't instantly think of gay culture. While it's true that Budapest is not Rio de Janeiro or Sydney in terms of its gay scene, there is a gay population that is on the rise in the city, and they make their presence known each year at the annual Budapest Pride festival, which typically takes place every July, and the highlight is a huge parade with lots of colourful floats winding through the streets of the city. This is a wonderful celebration to be part of, whether you are gay or not.

(http://budapestpride.com)

47. Eat Langos at Feny Street Market

Budapest has a wonderful market culture, and one of the most popular markets is Feny Street Market. This particular market is popular for two reasons: its variety of organic produce and its delicious langos. But what exactly are langos? These are a local type of flatbread that are really popular on the Budapest streets. It is typically served with sour cream and grated cheese on top, and it's particularly satisfying in the city's winter months.

(Lövőház u. 12; www.fenyutcaipiac.hu)

48. Discover Budapest's Gay scene at Alterego Club

When you think of gay party places in Europe, Budapest probably isn't the first city that pops into your head. And while Budapest still has a way to go before fully accepting its LGBT community, there is certainly a gay community in the city – and they know how to party! You can enjoy the best of Budapest's gay scene for yourself at Alterego

Club. It opens every Friday and Saturday night, with pop hits playing from the DJ booth, and drag shows to boot. *(Dessewffy u. 33; www.alteregoclub.hu)*

49. Meet People on a Budapest Pub Crawl

To get under the skin of Budapest, you really need to understand where people drink in their free time, and how they drink. Of course, you could amble around and visit any of the bars and pubs littered around, but you won't be assured that you are visiting the best places. A much better idea is to join one of the many Budapest pub crawls that exist in the city. You'll be taken to a variety of drinking establishments, taught about local spirits, and you'll make friends along the way!

(http://pubcrawl-budapest.com)

50. Learn About the City's Gruesome History at the House of Terror

Central and Eastern Europe certainly has ups and downs in its history, and Hungary is no exception. If you want to learn more about the fascist and communist regimes of Hungary in the 20th century, the House of Terror is the place to get educated. A particularly gruesome aspect of the museum is an exhibition that shows how the country's rulers would break the nerve of its prisoners through torture techniques.

(Andrássy út 60; www.terrorhaza.hu)

51. Explore the Danube River by Boat

One of the most iconic sites in all of Hungary is without a doubt the River Danube. Of course, there are all kinds of tour companies offering glitzy river cruises, but if you're on a budget, you should know that you can explore the river using Budapest's public transport system as well. Boats leave on the river every 20 minutes or so, and the price for the whole journey is under 2 euros.

52. Buy Original Photography at Vintage Galeria

Budapest has a thriving arts culture, and it can be a great idea to take out a couple of days just to visit the galleries in the city. An up and coming photography gallery is Vintage Galeria, and as well as being able to view the works of local artists, you can buy a lot of the work too. An original photograph from a local artist sure beats a souvenir from a tourist shop on the high street, right? There's also a small bookshop on the premises where you can find cool art and photography books for coffee tables.

(Magyar u. 26; http://vintage.hu)

53. Take in a Folk Dance Show at the Danube Palace

For a taste of local culture, Danube Palace, a Neo Baroque 19th century building, is 100% the place to be. To be honest, virtually any show here is going to be world class, but something to look out for is a folk dance performance from the Danube Folk Ensemble. This troupe has been putting on shows for Budapest crowds since the 1950s, with a dance group of 30 people and a musical band of 7. They stage over 100 performances a year, so there is no excuse not to catch one of their shows.

(Zrínyi u. 5; http://dunapalota.hu)

54. Check Out the City's Captivating Street Art

While Budapest is certainly known as a cultural city, it's mostly associated with grand concerts and blockbuster art exhibitions. But what of its underground arts culture?

Walk through District 7 and you will be blown away by the amount of street art on the city's walls, and many of the pieces are political in tone. If you want to understand more about the street art culture in the city, it can be a great idea to take one of the guided tours that explains Budapest's street art culture.

55. Take in a Budapest Panorama With a Drink at 360 Bar

There is no debating that Budapest is a beautiful city, but looking at the city from a street view is just one way of appreciating the beauty of Budapest. For a totally different view, be sure to order a drink at 360 Bar at sunset. This rooftop terrace offers a full 360 degree panorama of the city, which is particularly special during the sunset hour. Stick around because there is often live music playing on the roof as well.

56. Explore the Fascinating History of Budapest at Castle Museum

Want to get to grips with the history of the city? Look no further than the Castle Museum, which contains objects that are up to 40,000 years old! There are archaeological artefacts, objects of art, clothing from ancient Budapest, and loads more historical goodies that history and culture geeks will eat right up.

(Andrássy út 39; http://360bar.hu)

57. Party All Night in Thermal Baths

You have no doubt already heard about Budapest's thermal baths. These are a great place to relax your weary muscles, but even better, they are places where you can party too. The key is knowing where the best parties are. Lukacs Baths are an awesome choice, and they throw their Magical Bath Parties from October to April. You can expect pumping sounds, an incredible multimedia visual display, lots of beautiful people, and, of course, piping hot water from the baths.

(http://lukacsbaths.com)

58. Embrace Your Inner Carnivore at a Sausage Festival

Central and Eastern Europe is certainly partial to a sausage or two, and Budapest is no exception. Every year, a Palinka (Hungarian brandy) and sausage festival is hosted in the spectacular surrounds of Buda castle. There are many different kinds of delicious sausages to be tried in Hungary, some mild, some spicy, some cured, some dried – and so this is a great opportunity for meat lovers to really chow down on what Budapest has to offer.

59. Party in a 19th Century Palace With Hello Baby

Heading to Budapest with the express purpose of partying all night with the locals? We don't blame you because Budapest has an *epic* party scene to rival any other city in Europe. And a unique place to get your rocks off is every Friday and Saturday night with club organisers Hello Baby. They stage parties in the 19th century Haggenmacher Palace, which certainly beats your local dive bar. There is intricate design, balustrades, and lots of beautiful people – so you'll feel fit to party like royalty.

(Andrássy út 52; www.hellobabybar.hu)

60. Sip on Yummy Beers at Élesztő Craft Beer Garden

There's absolutely no shortage of places to drink on the streets of Budapest, but if you are a beer lover, head straight for the good stuff in the Eleszto Craft Beer Garden. Word on the street is that this place is the epicentre of the Hungarian beer revolution. You'll find lagers, bitters, ales, stouts, and more, mostly from Hungarian microbreweries. And as the name would suggest, this place has a beautiful garden space where you can relax and soak up some rays in Budapest's summer sunshine.

(Tűzoltó u. 22; www.elesztohaz.hu)

61. Buy Awesome Vintage Clothes at Iguana

Iguana is the kind of vintage clothing store that you'd expect to see on the streets of Brooklyn. There are a just a couple of differences – it's in Budapest, and the prices are a fraction of what you'd pay in the States. There is both menswear and womenswear, plus there's homeware and miscellaneous objects like bicycles and furniture too. If you have an eye for style and love a bargain, don't miss Iguana.

(Krúdy Gyula u. 9)

62. Make Your Stomach Happy During Budapest Restaurant Week

Without a doubt, one of the best things that you can do in Budapest is eat. And it's during the city's Restaurant Week, held in October each year, that you can really appreciate the incredible dining scene in the capital. Over 30 restaurants in the city take part in this gastronomic event, each offering a 3 course fixed menu with its signature dish for an extremely low price of around 10 euros. This is the week to be in Budapest for foodies who don't want to break the bank sampling delicious plates of local food.

63. Have the Local Budapest Experience With Couchsurfing

When you're in Budapest, you'll certainly want to take in the main tourist attractions, but this doesn't really teach you about how local people in the city actually live day-to-day. To get the real local experience, it's a great idea to sign up to Couchsurfing.com and instead of staying at a hotel or hostel, actually stay in the home of a local person – and all for free. While this is a great way to save money, the real benefit comes from the cultural exchange you will experience.

(www.couchsurfing.com)

64. Try a Slice of Dobos Cake at Daubner

Daubner might well be the busiest pastry shop in all of Budapest, and with good reason. Step inside and you'll be overwhelmed by the choices of pastries and cakes, but we'll make things easy for you and tell you to go straight for a slice of Dobos cake or Dobos torte. This delectable dessert features thin layers of sponge cake sandwiched together with rich chocolate butter cream, and there is a crunchy layer of hard caramel on the top. Yum!

(Szépvölgyi út 50; http://daubnercukraszda.hu)

65. Learn About Local Architecture at the Budapest 100 Festival

When you arrive in Budapest, something that will become immediately obvious is the beauty of the architecture and buildings in the city. Every April, Budapest 100 is a festival that celebrates the beauty, history, and grandeur of buildings over 100 years old. Buildings taking part include schools, residential houses, offices, and museums that are ordinarily closed to the public but open their doors for one weekend only, and free tours are offered in each district where there are participating buildings.

66. Learn How to Cook Hungarian Food Like a Local

Needless to say, on your trip to Budapest, you should be chowing down on lots of local fare. But how cool would it be if you didn't just eat the food, but actually learned how to make it so you could create a taste of Budapest in your own kitchen? There are numerous restaurants and cooking schools across the city that offer cooking classes but one of the best is definitely Culinary Hungary Cooking Class. First you'll be taken to a local market to buy your ingredients, and then you'll cook with your classmates in a real Budapest home.

(Forint u. 3; http://budapestcookingclass.com)

67. Grab a Bargain at the Ecseri Flea Market

Are you the kind of person who loves to shop for a bargain? If so, you should waste no time on your trip to

Budapest and head straight to the Ecseri Flea Market, which takes place at a location around 40 minutes from the centre (which means you won't be competing with many other tourists for the best swag!). You can find anything and everything there - homewares, vintage stamps, collectable artwork, and lots more. And haggling is standard, so remember to negotiate a good price!

(Nagykőrösi út 156; www.ecseripiac-budapest.hu)

68. Discover a Church Inside a Cave

Budapest has lots of beautiful churches but none is more unique than the church that is located inside a cave underneath Buda Hill. This church dates back to 1926 and was founded by a hermit monk who used the thermal waters of Budapest to cure local sick people. The small church has natural rock walls, and it's a cosy and quiet place to find some peace and tranquillity inside the city.

69. Have a Unique Wine Tasting Experience in Buda Castle

Let's face it – an evening of wine tasting in Budapest is never going to be a terrible night. But it becomes extra special when your wine tasting is located inside a cellar in Buda Castle, probably the most famous and grand building in the city. At Faust Wine Cellar, the staff are truly passionate about Hungarian wine, and you'll be able to taste wines from all 22 wine producing regions of the country. Just be sure to book your place ahead of time! *(http://gbwine.eu/index.php/en)*

70. Be Wowed by Hungarian Artefacts at the Museum of Applied Arts

To experience the traditional arts and crafts culture of Budapest and Hungary, the Museum of Applied Arts (which happened to be the 3rd oldest applied arts museum in the world) is a must visit on your trip. The collection is astoundingly impressive with artefacts such as Tiffany glassware, Hungarian folk ceramics that is centuries old, Ottoman carpets, and Baroque gold jewellery.
(Üllői út 33-37; www.imm.hu)

71. Say Hi to a Legend at the Michael Jackson Memorial Tree

Yes, you read correctly: there is, indeed, a tree dedicated to the memory of Michael Jackson in Budapest. It's located just across the road from Kempinski Hotel Corvinus because Jacko stayed there three times on trips to the city. There are pictures attached to the tree, messages of goodwill, and candles surrounding the tree as well. It's worth a visit for the novelty factor even if you aren't the hugest Michael Jackson superfan.

72. Eat Chips & Dips After a Night of Partying

Every destination around the world has its own version of Drunk Food. In Budapest, when the bars and clubs start to close, everybody heads for Chips & Dips in the party district. This place is famous for serving up three things. All of which, of course, are deep fried. There are good old fashioned French fries, potato rostis, and onion rings. And as the name of the joint would suggest, there are plenty of delectable dips to choose from too.

(Dob u. 18)

73. Decorate Pottery at MadeByYou

The fine porcelain of Budapest may be world famous, but if your budget doesn't quite extend to taking home a piece of collectable porcelain, you can still have fun with pottery in Budapest by joining a workshop at MadeByYou! All you have to do is turn up and they will supply all the materials and guidance you need to paint your own ceramics. What a super cool way to pass a rainy afternoon in the Hungarian capital city!

(Királyi Pál u. 11; www.madebyyou.hu)

74. Sip on Palinka, the Spirit of Budapest

Europe is an awesome place to get your booze on and each country has its own specialty tipple. Of course, Portugal is famous for port, and Poland is famous for vodka. In Budapest, you can find Palinka, but this is a little known spirit outside of Hungary that you might not even have heard of before. You can ask for this in virtually every Budapest bar, and it's a type of fruit brandy that can be made from many types of fruits, including plums, peaches, apricots, and apples. It's particularly warming in the winter months.

75. Peek at Budapest's Communist Era Statues

Budapest has a somewhat bleak 20th century history, with its fascist and communist regimes. It can be difficult to find traces of that time in the city centre, and, in fact, all of the Communist-era statues have been banished from the city and exist in the suburbs in Memento Park. Here you will be able to find Lenin, Marx, Engels, and variety of other Communist leaders.

(Balatoni út - Szabadkai utca saro; www.mementopark.hu)

76. Try Extreme Ice Cream Flavours at Vari

On a warm summer's day in Budapest, there is nothing more appealing than strolling the streets with a cone of ice cream. There are plenty of places to grab a creamy gelato in Budapest, but for some ice cream flavours with a difference, try out Vari Cukraszda. The chilli cocoa flavour is for somebody who likes spices, while the beetroot ice cream is surprisingly delicious. Whichever flavour you choose, you'll definitely be back for a second scoop.

(Szlovák út 86; www.varicukraszda.hu)

77. Leave Your Own Mark on a Budapest Pub

There are plenty of great places in Budapest for a piping hot bowl of goulash and a delicious Hungarian beer, but the For Sale Pub (yes, that's the name of the pub) is something a little bit special. The unique selling point here is that every customer is invited to leave their own stamp on the walls of the cellar pub. Small notes cover every inch of the walls, ranging from miniature paintings to photographs to handwritten memos. How will you leave your mark on this Budapest institution?

(Vámház krt. 2)

78. Learn Silk Screen Printing

If you are the kind of person who finds it hard to relax and unwind on a trip away, you may want to fill your days with fun activities rather than ambling from café to café. In which case, you should check out the silkscreen printing workshop at Budapest based Printa. You'll be given all the tools you need to create your own original print from scratch, resulting in a print that you can take home with you, creating a memory of your time in Budapest that lasts forever.

(Rumbach Sebestyén u. 10)

79. Check out the City's Musical Fountain

Over on Margaret Island, you can check out one of Budapest's most famous and enchanting attractions – the musical fountain! There are shows throughout the day when classical and pop music plays out of the fountain, and at the same time, 10 metre jets of water shoot up into the air! Be sure to check out one of the night shows when the fountain becomes illuminated at the same time as it pumps out the tunes.

80. Eat Lots of Yummy Palacsinta

Yes, there is yet more deliciousness to be consumed in Budapest! If you are not familiar with palacsinta, your trip to Budapest is the time to become acquainted. Palacsinta is essentially the Hungarian version of a thin crepe, and you'll want to consume more than a few of these if you have a sweet tooth. Some of the fillings for palacsinta are really unique; you can try candied orange peel, rum, sour cherry jam, cottage cheese, poppy seeds, and more besides. The pancake is then dished up with a chocolate sauce.

81. Learn Some Hungarian at a Language School

If you're only in Budapest for a couple of days, picking up the Hungarian language is probably not an option for you (although, even then, mastering "please" and "thank you" isn't such a big ask) but if you are planning to stick around for a longer stretch of time, you should definitely arrange to have some formal lessons in the Hungarian language in one of the city's language schools. By doing so, you'll graduate from simple tourist to someone who can communicate with locals on a much deeper level.

82. Catch a Puppet Show at the Budapest Puppet Theatre

If you fancy catching a local show in Budapest but you are worried about the hurdles of the Hungarian language, a fun show that you'll be able to understand without a problem is one from the Budapest Puppet Theatre. Budapest actually has a long tradition in puppetry and this puppet theatre company is 60 years old. This is a great way of entertaining young children and getting them to understand the local culture without dragging them around museums they don't want to go to.

(Andrássy út 69; www.budapest-babszinhaz.hu)

83. Listen to Hungarian Folk Music at Potkulcs

On a visit to Budapest, it's time to give your iPod a rest and open your ears up to some different forms of traditional Hungarian music. One of the most fun places to listen to some Hungarian tunes is at Potkulcs. This popular hang-out spot has a relaxed, local, bohemian crowd who love nothing more than to kick back and listen to the live Hungarian folk music that is more often than not playing. There's also a garden, which is ideal for taking in some cool air during the Budapest summer.

(Csengery u. 65b; www.potkulcs.hu/index.php?lg=en)

84. Enjoy a Circus Spectacular at Budapest City Circus

What's more fun than a trip to the circus?! If you love the spectacle of magic tricks, acrobats, and other awesome feats of the human body and mind, you are not going to want to miss the Budapest City Circus on your trip. The shows are located inside the famous City Park, and this troupe's origins can be dated all the way back to the 18th century! If you can't get enough of jugglers and trapeze artists, you might even want to try out the International Circus Festival, which is hosted every other February in the city.

(www.fnc.hu/eng)

85. Splash Around at Aquaworld

If you happen to be in Budapest during the summer months, it can be a great idea to cool off at the city's only water park, Aquaworld. It is, in fact, one of the largest indoor water parks in all of Europe, with 17 pools in total, a wave pool, a surf pool, pools with diving boards, lots of slides, and areas that young kids can enjoy as well.

(Ives Ut 16; www.aquaworldresort.hu/en)

86. Ride on a 100 Year Old Carousel at Vidampark

Vidampark is a local amusement park in the city, and it's perfect for a day out if you are travelling with children. There are many highlights inside the park, including a rickety roller coaster made of wood, and other rides, but the #1 attraction has to be the carousel, which is now 100 years old! From the top, you will have a spectacular vista of Budapest city.

87. Enjoy Hungarian Dishes With a Twist at Tanti Restaurant

Hungarians sure do know how to eat, and while you are in Budapest, it's a great idea to treat yourself at a few of the city's more upscale dining establishments. Tanti is the newest restaurant in Budapest with a Michelin star, and it's with good reason. The three course lunch is very affordable at just around 13 euros, and when you consider the quality of the food, it's quite unbelievable. Do not leave before you try the Mangalitza (a local type of pig) cheek with savoy cabbage.

(Apor Vilmos tér 11-12; www.tanti.hu)

88. Embrace Your Inner Teen at a Skate Park

When was the list time that you strapped on a pair of roller blades? Maybe not since your teenage years. But all that could change at the Gorzenal Skate Park. This is the #1 place in the city where local teens come to spin on their skate boards, roller blades, and BMX bikes – but they also offer roller blade rentals in the park. If you have a free afternoon, why not test out your skills?

(Gorzenal Skate Park; http://gorzenal.hu)

89. Down a Chilled Beverage at Budapest's Icebar

To be honest, Budapest's winter temperatures are cold enough so that an Ice bar isn't especially necessary, but if you want to experience the coolness of this bar in the summer, it's well worth the visit. Everything in the bar – the walls, the chairs, the bar, and even your glass – is made from ice and ice only. The bar is kept at a temperature of -5 degrees at all times, so if you like your drinks chilled, this is the place to be.

(Váci u. 82; www.icebar.hu)

90. Take Back a Souvenir of Tour Trip From Memories of Hungary

You might think that souvenir shops are an obvious thing to suggest and they aren't anything special, but the memories of Hungary shop is honestly a cut above the rest, and if you need to buy a selection of gifts, this is the place to get your shopping done. Instead of cheap factory made items, this souvenir shops specialises in handmade crafts made by local people. Some of the items you might want to buy include exquisite local porcelain and handmade textiles.

(Hercegprímás u. 8; http://memoriesofhungary.hu)

91. Discover Asian Art in Eastern Europe

Ferenc Hopp was a guy who travelled the world and was fascinated by Asiatic art. The Hopp Museum of East Asia Art is his very own personal collection, which comprises some 23,000 items from places as far flung as Japan, China, Nepal, and Mongolia. If you want a temporary respite from neo-gothic architecture and East European beers, this is the museum for something a little bit different.

(Andrássy út 103)

92. Check out Budapest Made From Marzipan

If you love nothing more than to take in information on random, niche topics, you will fall head over the heels for the Marzipan Museum, which, as you might have guessed, is dedicated to the wonders of marzipan. You won't learn a whole lot about marzipan itself, but you'll be wowed by marzipan that is manipulated into famous Budapest landmarks and fairy tale figures. This is one that the kids will really love!

(Hess András tér 1-3; www.szabomarcipan.hu/index.php?lang=en)

93. Take a Romantic Walk Along the Danube Promenade

Without a shadow of a doubt, Budapest is one of the most romantic cities on the planet, and something that every visiting couple can and should do, regardless of their budget, is take a romantic stroll along the river Danube's promenade. You'll have the opportunity to take in many important buildings, such as the Vigado Concert Hall and the Hungarian Academy of Sciences, and you can take in the ambience while you look at the flickering lights reflected in the water.

94. Eat Until You're Stuffed at the Great Market Hall

If you love to eat, you are in the right place, because Budapest is most definitely a destination for foodies. And if you want to chow down on lots of stuff all at once, the Great Market Hall is the very best place to do that. In fact, this is the largest indoor market in the whole city. Walk around from stall to stall, and start eating. You'll find big bowls of goulash being served up, stalls selling langos (local flatbreads), and spices, preserves, and pickles that you can take home with you.

(Vámház krt. 1-3)

95. Ascend to Budapest's Highest Peak: Elizabeth's Lookout

Budapest is a stunning city, but to really take in all of the city's beauty, you have to view it from a height. The highest lookout point in all of the city is called Elizabeth's Lookout at 526 metres in height and it was built in 1911. When the weather is clear, you'll, actually see far beyond the city and you might even be able to view the Matra Mountains, which are 80 kilometres away, so check the weather forecast before you make the ascent!

96. Visit One of the Oldest Zoos in the World

If you're travelling with kids, or just want a day out of the city, a trip to the zoo is always a great idea. And Budapest Zoo and Botanical Garden is one of the oldest and most impressive zoos in the world, having opened its doors for the first time in 1866. There's more than 1000 species of animals in the zoo, including the impressive Komodo Dragon, and an incredibly diverse selection of primates. *(Állatkerti krt. 6-12; www.zoobudapest.com)*

97. Check out Contemporary Dance at the Central European Dance Theatre

Budapest is the kind of city that most people visit in order to experience its traditions. Wonderful as they are, if you want a spot of contemporary culture, you can't do much better than to take in a contemporary dance performance at the Central European Dance Theatre. This was actually the first independent dance theatre in Hungary, and it continues a legacy to stage innovative, independent dance from Hungary and internationally.

98. Take in an Art House Movie at Cinema Puskin

Sometimes all you want to do is relax while watching a great movie. Instead of going to a regular cinema, you need to head to the very best in Budapest – Cinema Puskin, a cinema that specialises in showing cutting edge art house movies. It's been showing pictures since 1926, and it's worth a visit for the beauty of the old-school cinema interior itself, which makes watching a film seem like the most decadent experience in the world.

(Kossuth Lajos u. 18; http://puskinmozi.hu)

99. Try Hungary's Answer to Trifle: Somlói Galuska

Yup, there is yet more deliciousness to be sampled in Budapest, and this time in the form of Somlói Galuska, which is Hungary's version of a trifle. It is made with three different layers of sponge cake, rasins, walnuts, cream, chocolate sauce, and rum. Long story short – it's heaven on a plate, and you'd be a fool not to fill your stomach with it on a trip to Budapest.

100. Visit a Pinball Museum

Okay, the Pinball Museum of Budapest may not be the most well known attraction in the city, nor at the top of your "must visit" list, but if you have some free time and an appreciation for old arcade games, it's definitely worth checking it out. The best thing about this place is that the pinball machines are kept under lock and key, but you can actually play with all 130 pinball machines, the oldest of which dates back to 1871. Pretty cool!

(Radnóti Miklós u. 18; www.flippermuzeum.hu/en)

101. Get in Touch with Nature at the Tropicarium

Budapest's aquarium is one of the most impressive in all of Europe, including a freshwater, open air aquarium that changes with the seasons and is home to many local species. But if you are looking for something a little more exotic, make sure you are at the Tropicarium at 3pm on Thursdays when there is a live feeding of the sharks!

(Nagytétényi 37-43; http://tropicarium.hu/en)

Before You Go...

Thanks so much for reading **101 Amazing Things to Do in Budapest**. We really hope that this helps to make your time in Budapest the most fun and memorable trip that it can be.

Have a great trip!

Team 101 Amazing Things

Printed in Great Britain
by Amazon